ANCIENT WARS:
Sexuality and Oppression

by

Ethna Viney

ETHNA VINEY is a writer and journalist and a regular contributor to *The Irish Times*. She lives in Co. Sligo.

1

This pamphlet is dedicated to all those who have continued the thankless struggle to bring enlightenment, equality and a place in the sun to all women.

First published in 1989 by
Attic Press
44 East Essex Street
Dublin 2

British Library Cataloguing in Publication Data
Viney, Ethna
  Ancient wars - sex and sexuality.
  1. Man. Sexuality - Sociological perspectives
  1. Title
  306.7

ISBN 0-946211-83-3

Cover Design: Paula Nolan
Typesetting: Attic Press
Printing: Elo Press

INTRODUCTION

When you stop to think about it, the extent to which sexuality rules a woman's existence is remarkable. Ever present in her adult life is evidence of her sexuality - the physical evidence of menstruation, contraception or pregnancy, childcare; and more abstractly, importunate love (romantic or lustful) and the price she has got to pay for its satisfaction - a lifetime of service unless she struggles against her fate. There are the obvious, despotic effects of sexuality, and ones that society considers "natural" - hard luck on women, and all that. If, however, women are to do something about their inequality then they must understand the reasons for it. These reasons are not simple; and they emerge from a culture of ancient lineage, which is full of misconceptions and prejudices. To express or articulate criticism of this culture is to be called "manhating", (for, as we all know, it is a male culture), and it is impossible to avoid the slander, from both women and men, if one writes about the structure and component parts of women's inequality. The problem is that many women accept men's warped perception of womankind, or refuse to see the elements of oppression in it, either because the realisation would be too hard to bear, or they insulate themselves within the cocoon of a personal relationship which is satisfactory for them.

Sexuality is a subject not easily or readily discussed in Ireland; and when the word is used it takes on a variety of meanings. For the purposes of this pamphlet, and so that we all know what we mean, I use the word 'sexuality' in its dictionary definition of relations between the sexes, especially with reference to mutual attraction and to gratification of resulting desires. I intend to use both parts of this definition, and to show that the wider interpretation of 'relations between the sexes' - the general acts and attitudes of men towards women because they are women, and women towards men because they are men - is considerably influenced by the narrower one of sexual attraction and activity. It could be said that this is encroaching on the territory of the word 'gender', which means the cultural characteristics of the sexes, and around which a controversy - "Is gender biological or is it cultural?"- rages. However, gender is rooted in sexuality and I intend to show that sexuality is not only biological, but that it is also heavily cultural and governs the way the sexes treat each other. I also intend to show that while the high point of male sexuality is penetration and ejaculation, the climax of women's sexuality is the earth-shattering orgasm of giving birth, the Big O.

CULTURE

Our culture envelops us like an old and comfortable coat - no, more like a warm familiar room. It is hallowed by living, dear to us as part of our routine and our past, it is right. We are slow to change its organisation, because that is the way it has always been; we are used to the arrange-

4

ment. It can exist side by side with change, new ideas and the search for truth. During periods of change, we cling to large portions of our culture, even the awkward or useless bits, almost unconsciously, because it is familiar. It gives us social stability and security, and a framework for our lives. By culture I mean not just art and literature, but a broader context of the customs, practices and beliefs of the society in which we live: the way we communicate with each other; our working habits and liesure pursuits; religion, politics; how we solve problems and celebrate success; in a word, our attitudes to everything.

Culture is absorbed by all of us, as we grow up and as we grow older, from the society in which we live. The process of socialisation could be called "conditioning", or more pejoratively "brainwashing", but I prefer to call it "internalising": we take in ideas and attitudes from the prevailing culture and make them our own, internalise them. I prefer that term because we cooperate, indeed concur, with the process, and it is therefore something over which we can exercise control. Debriefing oneself, however, is not easy; you need an overriding drive to do so. Even after a successful debriefing flashes of the old conditioning can return like the hallucinogenic relapses experienced by drug addicts.

Rooted deep within our culture is an attitude to women which can only be described as misogyny, a degrading and a downgrading of women, which is based on their sexuality. In the course of this pamphlet I will make some tough criticism of our culture, of male culture, of men who maintain it and of the support we women give it. Many women will say that the men they know are not fiends who degrade or oppress women. They may be right. Some men do not; and it is likely that many of the women who are concerned about the problem of oppression, and who will read this text, will tend to know and favour those men who treat women with fairness. Indeed the oppressors and the degraders avoid engagement with women who challenge their position, or read pamphlets like this; they give them a wide berth when seeking a 'wife' or female companion. At the same time, let us not forget that even the fairest of men do little to challenge the prevailing culture which is the medium through which the subordination of women works.

For those who do not believe that there is a deeply ingrained streak in our culture that defines and degrades women in terms of their sexuality, I will recount an incident which happened to a friend of mine last summer. She was taking the bus from Heuston railway station to the centre of Dublin, and alongside her bus stood another, full of ten-year-old girls on a school outing. Seated behind her on the bus were two yobbos who carried on a conversation in revolting detail about the pleasures of raping these school girls when they were ten years older. It is immaterial whether they really meant what they said, or whether they were merely chest-thumping for each other's benefit: they had the ideas and the vocabulary of sexual oppression, and a cultural context in which to express them.

5

SEXUALITY IN IRELAND

We are a society ambivalent about sexuality - we have celibate priests, a religion which forbids pre-marital sex and until the recent past, had generations of bachelors. Sexual expression is so narrowly confined to what is known as "the sex act" or "sexual intercourse", which is penile penetration of the vagina, that other expressions of sexuality such as affectionate touching and kissing are virtually dismissed; they are marginalised. This was not always the case. In the importunate youth of half the population of this country (the older half) - before the advent of the permissive society, the Pill and commonplace pre-marital sex - sexual expression took a form which ranged from mild affectionate touching, such as holding hands, to heavy petting which stopped short of "the sex act".

Now male readers from that era will dispute the virtues of that period. They will tell of the pain of thwarted passion. But did they not talk themselves up to that passion in the first place? Did the passion not often start in competitive, macho male conversations; and did expectations not also play a major part in the arousal of these passions?

In Ireland, in the second half of this century, cultural attitudes to sexuality have undergone change. From the days of parish priests beating the hedgerows for courting couples when sex outside marriage was the paramount sin, and of women being castigated in confession for refusing intercourse to their husbands, there is now a somewhat more rational view of this human condition and its functions. However, with some people, a certain amount of prurience still attaches to the subject, a hangover from the severe repression of those bygone days. At the same time the state, on behalf of society, and even more so, the Catholic Church, try to regulate women's sexuality by controlling their fertility; there is legislation limiting the use of contraceptives, and an article in the Constitution forbidding the introduction of legislation relating to abortion. The Contraception Debate and the Abortion Referendum are the nearest this country has ever got to a long overdue discussion of sexuality; and these subjects are merely symptoms of a very narrow interpretation of what sexuality is really about.

Feminists are taking a close, sharp look at the role of women in our society, at their inferior status and oppression in a world of male supremacy, and at their apparent acquiescence in this situation. Are we oppressed because we are of the female sex, or because we are physically weaker? If the latter, why has there not been a mass rebellion in the ages when weapons provide an equaliser? And if being female is the reason, has it to do with our gender, which is the sum of our womanly characteristics; or is it because of our sexuality, our particular hormonal make-up and our ability to bear and feed children? Are men, perhaps, really superior?

What have feminists found in their quest for truth? They found that the roots of our oppression lie deep in our culture and in our psyches. It has been learned and imposed, assimilated and internalised, and condenses into a simplistic message: *men have needed to believe that they are superior to women, and we have been brainwashed into believing it too.* (If you don't believe that you have been brainwashed, ask yourself why you feel contempt for a man who dresses as a woman, and not for a woman who dresses as a man.) Our consent to this state of affairs has been obtained by socialisation which starts from the moment we are born and which operates through the components of our early small world - parents and friends, teachers, books and pictures, toys and clothes; and later on through the mass media (including advertising), and professionals such as doctors and psychologists. A few women, and fewer men, have gone some distance in debugging their minds; but overwhelmingly life rolls on with the caste of women regarded as inferior to the caste of men. Why?

Let's look first at our culture as it depicts and affects us, women and men. It is, in fact, two cultures, a pair of twins, complementary but not identical. The nature of women's culture is regarded as passive, weak, emotional, caring, helpful, co-operative, valuing friendship, not into dominating others, life-giving, inferior. Although some exceptions are allowed, women who depart from this image suffer disapproval or even punishment. Men's culture, on the other hand, is regarded as assertive, strong, unemotional, hierarchical, independent, death-dealing, superior. Again exceptions are allowed, but men who do not conform are generally despised. These different characteristics are regarded by the culture as given, and from them are derived the roles allotted. Women are the child-rearers, homemakers, servers and servicers; men are the providers, protectors, lawmakers: man, head; woman, heart.

Women's re-evaluation of themselves and of their culture is part of a process that has been going on for more than a century. Unfortunately, because feminism suffers generational recessions, at every re-emergence of their movement women must again "reinvent the wheel". Over the past twenty years, in the current cycle of feminism, this process has been occurring in stages. Stage one began when women looked for equal rights with men, and found that control of their own fertility was essential. In stage two women started to invade the "male world". This meant adopting a male value system which did not always rest comfortably on their shoulders. It also meant doing two jobs because men did not make any significant attempt to enter the "female realm". Stage three is the cultural struggle now in progress, or more precisely in the process of discussion, which is women consolidating their own value system, accepting some values from "male culture" and discarding others. Stage four will be designing a new culture, a revolutionary concept for women to undertake because it means redesigning personal lives and relationships.

For the past twenty years wherever a Women's Movement emerged, the main preoccupation has been with sexual politics. The emphasis has been on one or other aspect of biological sexuality - women' fertility, the mechanics of sexuality, sexual abuse and violence towards women - and the narrow interpretation of sexual preference. Sexual politics cover all areas of women's exploitation. Women are exploited and oppressed because of their sex, because they are biologically different from men, and therefore, can be grouped, tagged and treated in a particular manner. Persecuting identifiable groups is a power tactic that occurs with depressing regularity in history, and most dramatically in instances of racism; in the case of the African and Red Indian peoples and many others in colonial times; and, closer in time and place, in the case of the Jews in Nazi Germany, Blacks in South Africa and current sectarian killings in Northern Ireland.

But why do men want to exploit women? Why do men ridicule women and usually in reference to their sexuality? *What is it in the essence of women, in their sexuality, that has aroused a misogyny and antagonism which stretches back through history?*

HISTORY OF MISOGYNY

A brief look back through human history reveals a strong, steely core of misogyny throughout the surviving records. The Old Testament of the Bible, the Homeric Epics and the Tables of Ancient Rome are among the oldest historical writings, and together with our own Annals are the foundation on which European culture (including ours) grew. The Old Testament begins with the story of Eve in the Garden of Eden, and continues with one account after another of the exploitation of women.

The story of Eve's role in "the Fall" has been used as a stick with which to beat women for at least four thousand years. Yet, a careful examination of the Bible shows Adam to be just as much to blame as Eve for their separate sins of disobedience. The Bible account does not say that she knocked him down and forced the apple into his mouth. He succumbed to temptation just as much as Eve did. If he was unable to resist the temptation, that was his fault. Where was his much vaunted superiority?

The Bible story of the Fall was interpreted by the early Church Fathers as an allegory in which partaking of the fruit from the tree of knowledge of good and evil was the discovery of sexuality, whereupon the eyes of Adam and Eve were opened and they knew that they were naked and they sewed fig leaves together to cover themselves. When God appeared, Adam ran whining to him: "It was all her fault. She gave me the apple." And He cursed both of them, laying sorrow and pain in childbirth on Eve because of her sexuality, and making her subordinate to Adam; and sentencing Adam to hard labour for his sexuality. For thousands of years po-faced priests, like Adam, have been laying blame on women, as daughters of Eve, for "the Fall", and for everything else that went wrong since then. Are men not sons of Eve, and women daughters of Adam? What has happened to logic?

8

The Bible is full of horrendous tales of the oppression and exploitation of women, and of a misogyny directly related to sexuality. For example, menstruating and post-natal women were (and in Jewish practice still are) considered unclean and unfit to enter the synagogue. Out of the hundreds of instances of disregard for and antagonism to women I will mention just two : Moses ordered the death of the sexually active (married) Midianite women captured in battle, and the sexual enslavement of the virgins (all males had been killed). Both Lot and the man of Gibeah sought to appease thugs who called at their houses seeking to sodomise their male guests, by offering their virgin daughters to them instead, to satisfy their lust. Few interpret the Old Testament literally. It is regarded as an amalgam of folklore and stories handed down by word of mouth and, more than likely, distorted from the original facts by the time that it came to be written. What is certain is that when it was written it reflected the culture of the time, a culture which has formed the basis of our own culture.

Jesus preached a kinder religion with equality for all believers whether women or men. In the persecuted Christian Church of the early centuries women were accepted as leaders, priests and teachers of congregations. But in every century there were powerful and articulate male leaders who kept alive the misogyny of the Old Testament and of the Hebrew tradition, from Paul, (who dipped his pen in his own brand of vitriol), Tertullian, Jerome and Ambrose to John Chrysostom and Augustine. They all had a pathological aversion to sexuality, for the existence of which they blamed women.

As Christianity spread over Europe, it encountered other cultures with traditions of subordinating women, thus reinforcing a tendency of its own which had never really disappeared. Before and during the early Christian period in Ireland, women were classed with captives, slaves and drunks as "senseless"; but in later centuries, and through to the end of the Middle Ages, Irish women, at least among the upper and educated classes (who kept the records), made political and legal gains - in property rights, equality in marrriage, the right to divorce - rights which were limited by Norman influence and ended by the advent, in the seventeenth century, of English law.

Meanwhile Thomas Aquinas, at the centre of Christian power during the Middle Ages, added his tuppenceworth to keep the pot boiling, with a contempt for women's sexuality that has poisoned our society ever since. He decreed that the power of grace could never be transmitted to the female creature. Hence, being female came first among the disabilities which automatically disqualified a person from the priesthood, before being insane, enslaved, a murderer, illegitimate or crippled. The resounding echo of his prejudice still rings loudly through the Christian churches today when the Pope and other Churchmen try lamely to justify their own prejudice and misogyny. The Council of Trent, which established the rule of clerical celibacy, did so to preserve the clergy from "the filth of impurity and unclean bondage". Women's sexuality is still being used to keep them out of positions of authority in the Roman Catholic Church, and to maintain a celibate clergy.

But, said Aquinas, if women took vows of chastity, and foreswore sex, pregnancy and childbirth, they could achieve the dignity of men. And many women of that period, those from the better-off families, followed that advice. They banded together in convents; not for the reasons the Church Fathers believed, I am sure, but to be free of the daily interference of men, to take charge of their own future and have dignity and honour.

They were the lucky ones; the women who didn't, and who were assertive, presumptuous or "uppity", became the object of the greatest wave of lethal misogyny, that ever swept Europe - the witch hunts of the fifteenth and succeeding centuries. *Malleus Malificarum* (Hammer of the Witches), a document drawn up by two Dominican priests at the behest of the Pope at the end of the fifteenth century, became a powerful instrument of woman hatred. It contained all the traditional condemnations of women, their inferiority, evil inclinations and uncleanness, and then linked them to witchcraft, sorcery, heresy and demonology.

Women were sexually insatiable, they said, they copulated with the Devil and he then gave them formulas for potions to cast spells on men. The two monks described in pornographic detail the orgies and lewdness of the witches' activities with the Devil, and their fevered imaginings led them into even greater paroxysms of hatred for women. During a period of two centuries following their endeavours, hundreds of thouands of women, perhaps more than a million, were tortured and killed.

Today someone exhibiting such mental antics would be termed psychopathic; and although to a large extent (except perhaps among fundamentalists) such demented fantasies have no public acceptance, the cultural attitudes that they encouraged remain. Paradoxically, in the two religions which evolved from Judaism and influenced attitudes to women in our hemisphere - Christianity and Islam - the founders intended equality for all followers. There are no texts in the Gospels of the New Testament or in the Koran calling for the suppression of women. In both religions the Patriarchs went back to the Old Testament for their authorisation, subverting the intentions of the Founders.

As in the centuries before the witch hunts, an unbroken tradition of misogyny can be traced through the social records of the intervening centuries. When women emerged from a period of severe oppression into one of comparative freedom, they may have thought that the improvement was permanent, as did the women of Iran before the fundamentalists took control. Historically, women's freedom has risen and fallen like the waves on the sea, or like the tides, making only imperceptible gains against the land with each flow and losing much of that gain at the ebb.

Take but one of the sexual oppressions visited on women - rape. As we have seen, it has impeccable, biblical provenance, an accepted history and it still flourishes. Considered feminist analysis sees rape as the product of male power, and its function the control of all women's sexuality by men. That is not a surprising conclusion when a successful act of intercourse is regarded in our culture as an effective remedy for female discontent. Many believe that a woman's psychic problems or unusual behaviour is a desire for rough sex ("a good fucking"). Once she has had it her exaggerated ideas will dissolve of their own accord.

It would seem at first glance that there are two types of rape: sex-inspired and power-inspired. But on closer examination power is at the core of both. The man who believes that a woman has been leading him on (a "cock-teaser"), rapes her partly because he is aroused but also to show "who is boss", to control her, to take revenge on her. Rape is a punishment for women who express their sexuality; and also for women who challenge men in what men consider their own areas of superiority. It can also be a simple declaration of man's superiority and power over women.

There are lesser examples of male control of women's sexuality which, in all societies, is surrounded by legal and cultural restraints. These are manifested in many different ways from Italian bottom-pinching to the chador of Islam; in the contempt for, and dismissal of, non child-bearing women - 'spinsters' and the old; in pornography and prostitution; coercive sex everywhere and laws regulating reproduction; the commercial use of women's bodies in advertising; in the inescapable promotion of sexuality and eroticism in pop music, films, advertising and pulp fiction. You will find it even in the nicknaming of Dublin's sculptures of women: "the floozie in the jacuzzi", "the tart with the cart", "the hag with the bag". Everywhere male sexuality is represented as dominant, female sexuality as passive and exploitable. Women's acceptance of this control is evident in the way that some have internalised it even at the expense of their health: for instance in the way they walk - hiding breasts in concave chests, walking from the thighs to keep their buttocks stationary. The free-striding, confident woman is a challenge to male pride and sexuality because he interprets her bearing as sexual, and he wants to suppress it.

In the midst of this sex-laden atmosphere, women must not be assertive, because their assertiveness is linked automatically to their sexuality and is seen as a challenge to men. "Keep your heads down, girls!" is the message. Male reaction has always been either the arrogant, "How dare such an inferior creature, whose functions are related to blood and guts, assert herself before the cleanness and integrity of my superior and cerebral person?" or the more aggressive "I'll show her who's boss; she needs a good fucking."

Dependency, deference, discrimination, derision, despotism, unpaid service, rape and violence are the continuing, camouflaged characteristics of relations between men and women. Some say that this astonishing edifice of misogyny, of antagonism, of disdain towards and exploitation of women arose from the desire of men to know their own children; and some say that it derives from the monopoly that women have on childrearing. Others claim that the problem is caused by envy of women's role in reproduction (wombenvy).

Most certainly, men's desire to know their children inspired actual, physical subjection of women; the only way men could be sure of knowing their own offspring was to hold the mothers in as close captivity as was practicable. Some researchers say that men resent the power that their mothers had over them in their infancy, and that they retaliate for that early impotence. If men were equally involved in child nurture, they say, then women would not be marked out for revenge.

The theory about womb-envy goes as follows: men, it says, invented war as an antidote to womb-envy, giving themselves a role more important than that of women in the community: its protection against annihilation. Women might be important to the continuation of the species, but their efforts would come to nought if they were wiped out by enemies. It is a persuasive idea. Since records began, men's history glorifies war and martial cultures; and women's history, the history of social civilisation, has been ignored. We have got the evidence of our own eyes that female subordination is taught, and then becomes accepted as natural - a hallowed tradition - which is reinforced by warfare. We also observe that men, and only men, are taught to be aggressive in ordinary life, and rigorously trained in aggression for war. Humans are the only species that have institutionalised hostilities against each other. There are easier ways for men to know their children and to offset womb-envy than by war and exploitation. If these two conditions are its side effects, it is time we examined human sexuality in greater detail.

HUMAN SEXUALITY

When the campaigners of the Irish Women's Movement (and also those in other countries) began their struggle in the early 1970s, they found that their demands for equality of status and opportunity led back to factors relating to their sexuality. Man-serving, child-bearing and rearing, and the structure of the family within which these occupations took place, were what kept women dependent and poor. And women bought their place within that structure with their sexuality.

That was one way of putting it. Another way to define the situation was to say that the role of women in life was to rear children and provide sexual and personal service to a man; and this was best achieved in the family structure. (One can only say that the desire of men to know their children seemed to be matched by the great biological drive in women to have children, and both perpetuated an exploitative family structure.)

These were harsh definitions. They took no account of romance or love, or of the fact that when people lived off the land, in a primitive, cashless, subsistence economy, equality was possible between men and women in the family. In the 20th century, economics had changed, and whatever way one looks at it, women lost out in the family situation, for when the rising tide of romantic love which swept them into it receded, they were like castaways on a desert island. Their responsibilities to their children (and in Ireland these were numerous) were as impassable as a trackless, craftless ocean. Rafts had to be built.

With great courage and daring, in 1971, fifty Irish women organised a trip by train from Dublin to Belfast to buy and bring back contraceptives which were then illegal in the Republic of Ireland. It was a public protest and carried out in a glare of media attention. The objective was to highlight the enslavement of women to a life of repeated pregnancies and the rearing of large families; and to show that the law banning contraceptives was hypocritical and affected mainly the poor. Many who could afford it travelled regularly to Belfast to buy supplies of contraceptives; and this traffic and illegal importation of banned goods was ignored by Irish Customs.

During the following years, one by one the issues emerged: contraception, divorce, abortion, sexual harassment, rape, violence. The Women's Movement found that resistance to equal pay and equal opportunity to, and at, work were also linked to women's sexuality. Her child-bearing and rearing, it was said, were factors that would interfere with a woman's ability to hold down a job outside the home; her child-bearing and rearing would suffer if she worked outside the home. That old biblical phobia, menstruation, was again trotted out; this time it was said to impair a woman's ability to do a proper job. These reasons for discriminating against women are not openly declared very often now; but that does not mean that they are not held. Women have at least, for the present, won a climate in which articulating such ideas attracts derision. But let's take a closer look at sexuality.

We owe our present ability to discuss and analyse sexuality to the Women's Movement of the past two decades. Society's attitudes towards women's sexuality, which includes the moral and censorious, the prurient and exploitative, make it difficult for women to discuss the subject, or even to find the right words in which to debate it, without sounding crude or technical. However, the consciousness-raising sessions of the 1970s, in which women explored the roots of their oppression, cleared the way for a clarity of language which must have shocked some. Since then, feminist thinkers have sought to tease out the biological from the cultural and social aspects of this human phenomenon.

If human sexuality were not beset by so many cultural agglutinations, it is likely that it could take its place as neither more nor less important, than some other pleasurable aspects of life, both physical and mental. Basic human needs (which are also pleasures) can be graded in three groups of declining importunity:
* hunger, thirst and warmth. These are essential for life and the survival of the individual;
* sexual activity, fitness, the activity impulse. These are of secondary importance, but necessary for the survival of the species and

13

important for the wellbeing of the individual;
* use of the senses, speech, achievement of purpose, appreciation of beauty. These enhance the life of the individual.

It is a monumental myth that sexuality as we know it - an imprisoned animal, partly domesticated, used and abused in a whole spectrum of ways and for a multitude of purposes, sometimes pathological, and sometimes out of control - is true human sexuality. Let us first look at the general perception of human sexuality.

At its most basic, and in its narrowest sense, human sexuality, like that of all mammals, exists in the interest of reproduction, but it has evolved and developed beyond its mammalian base just as, and because, humans have evolved. Sexual activity is now a social (and leisure) pursuit with economic connotations, as well as a biological phenomenon; it concerns intimacy as well as reproduction. Even the Roman Catholic Church accepts that matrimonial sexual activity, while primarily for reproduction, is also an exercise which is important to the happiness of the couple.

Human sexuality cannot be compared to the behaviour of other mammals principally because of the development of human intelligence and memory, but also because of other factors such as the psychological effects of our long childhood and the fact that we have contributed to our own evolution by the changes which we have made in our environment - the transcendence of humans, in which some would deny women a part. Other species procreate purely by instinct, but the human species has an awareness of its own continuity and a conscious interest in both its own past and the future of its progeny. The pleasure or relief from tension that induces other mammals to procreate in response to oestrus is also present in humans; but in humans these are urges that are controlled by their intelligence, not instincts to which they are blindly obedient. Their sexual encounters involve thoughts and feelings that are infinitely more complex than the instinctive coupling of other species.

Well, so far, there are no obvious reasons to be found, in the basic function of sexuality, as to whether, or why, it should be an instrument of women's oppression. The females of other species are not subjugated by the males; and sexual activity does not have the ever-present influence on their lives that it seems to have in the human species. The reasons must lie elsewhere, perhaps in the differences between the species, of which the principal one is intelligence.

Anthropologists, psychoanalysts and other behavioural scientists have been rummaging around in their fields of interest seeking explanations for male supremacy, and two main schools of thought have emerged, both based on human sexuality. The first is biological determinism. Because women and men have physically different reproductive systems, some behavioural scientists believe that they have other biological differences which are reflected in their characters. For example, man is aggressive and woman is passive; and therefore as man is physically stronger than woman, it is inevitable that she should be oppressed by him. This credo (which I shall return to later) relies heavily on human biology and instinct, and leaves no room for the role of intelligence in power relations between the sexes. It may well have female protagonists, but I have only come across its male proponents. And it raises the hackles of most women I know.

In the second school of thought, a growing number of scientists and philosophers hold that sexuality, (the relations between the sexes, as opposed to human relations which disregard sex), is socially and culturally constructed, that it is a series of attitudes and emotions which are learned, and that sexual activity, even the forms which reproductive sexual activity take (apart from the basic drive), are also learned. This conclusion is supported by masses of evidence, and it gives intelligence a central role in relations between the sexes.

In conventional wisdom, male sexuality is compulsive, aggressive, not necessarily linked to emotion. It goes further than that: men define their identity, their masculinity, in terms of their sexuality, and identify their sexuality with power and prestige. These are cultural imperatives. All over the world, there are cultural pressures for males to prove their masculine sexuality (to have balls), by being aggressive, not showing the gentler emotions, being sexually active, and aspiring to power (which in its least manifestation is the control of a woman), as evidence of their masculinity. Human culture allows men a very limited range of feelings and emotions in public; they can be angry, aggressive, courageous, competitive, exhilarated, arrogant, proud or imperious; all emotions that relate to ability, status and power. Above all they should not show fear, submission, or any of the softer feelings or caring emotions. These are not manly.

On the other hand, women's sexuality is regarded as passive, existing only as a response to male sexuality, related to emotion, and a trap for unwary men. There is a lot of doublethink on the question of women's sexuality. Side by side with this image of a quiescent libido, paradoxically, women are also supposed to be sexually insatiable (the arousal of a woman probably frightens men because, as will become evident later, it is outside their control). Their carnality is considered a danger to men, diverting them from higher things (note again the Eve syndrome); and everything to do with women's sexuality is regarded as dirty. By whom are these views held? Not overtly or consciously by the vast majority of us, women or men; but these attitudes run like a deep seam in human culture, and they submerge and resurface again at intervals throughout history. There are multitudes of records testifying to their existence, and one may think that they have disappeared in modern times in our developed society. But while sanitary pads are publicly displayed in supermarkets and magazine advertisements, menstruation is still regarded as if it were a guilty secret. Fertility and child-birth are messy considerations which women should confine among themselves (except for the lucrative practice of gynaecologists). A recent article in *The Irish*

Times recorded the antipathy of many men, even trade unionists and politicians, to married women of child-bearing years in the workforce. These revelations were followed by a letter in the same paper from a retired primary school teacher who recalled an incident in the 1960s when her principal, a nun, remarked to her about a pregnant married colleague, how inappropriate and unseemly morally it was for an obviously pregnant woman to stand in front of a class.

Only in the last two decades has the Roman Catholic Church abandoned the ritual of Churching (purifying) women after childbirth. And only over the same period has the custom of fathers attending the birth of their children become an accepted (if not general) practice. Celibacy among clergy and opposition to women priests rests on these same prejudices, as does the scandal attached to sexual dalliance by highly placed public figures.

This is where we come to the double standard in attitudes to women's and men's sexuality. There are different sets of rules for male and female sexual behaviour (as indeed in other areas of life): men are allowed to be sexually promiscuous, while women are not. Present day breaches of this bastion of male privilege are more apparent than real. Research has shown that women who have emulated the sexual behaviour of men find it personally unsatisfactory; while at the same time men retain their categorisation of women: those who sleep around are sluts, nice women don't.

The double standard has internal illogicalities, eg prostitutes are dirty. What makes them dirty? Men's penises. So why are men who go to prostitutes not dirty? Dorothy Dinnerstein, an American analyst, replies: *'The messiness allowed men in our own culture does not really contradict this point (that men are clean and women dirty). Their proverbial unfastidious lust, their tolerance of filthy public toilets, their foul language and slovenly ways, all of this is accepted because it does not touch upon their central, clean humanity. It is washed off, like dirt off healthy skin, when they turn to serious matters. In woman messiness of this kind would convey that an intrinsic, inherent uncleanliness, which she is counted to keep under control, has broken out of bounds'.*

THE SEXUAL REVOLUTION

Here, I'll give a brief tabulated account of two revolutions of recent decades - the sexual and the feminist:

1. Sexual radicalism, sleeping around, facilitated by the Pill, was the sexual revolution of the '60s. The Pill changed the character of the sexual revolution. The separation of intercourse from reproduction brought new freedom to women. It also brought benefits to men by releasing them from some responsibility for their sexual acts. Women soon realised that it was freedom only to say "yes", not to say "no"; they were "frigid" if they said no! This knowledge partly gave rise to the present wave of

feminism.

2. The role of motherhood and childcare, in keeping women economically dependent and deprived, became another issue. The key to men's control over women, they found, lay in their control of female sexuality and, as a direct consequence, women's domestic labour. Patriarchy (male dominance) was defined as the first and most basic aspect of all power relations; and the family came under attack.

3. Women came to realise that femaleness was defined by men; that they had adopted and internalised a male interpretation of their sexuality, and that purging themselves of it would be difficult. Even today definitions of female sexuality are still afflicted by the virus of male perceptions. At first women questioned the language and practice of sexuality which assigned activity and control to men, and passivity and surrender to women.

4. Next came anger against the beliefs, ideas and arrangements surrounding reproduction. Women's fertility, they found, and ultimately their lives, were in men's hands. They sought control of their own fertility - hence the demands for safe contraception and abortion. (They were still defining their sexuality in male terms). Health care became an issue and the question of authoritarian (mainly male) doctors.

5. Frigidity had engaged the interest of sexologists in the early years of the century. It was the diagnosis offered by men to women who failed to reach orgasm. Later they decided that virtuosity in sexual activity was the cure, and female satisfaction was made dependent on male resourcefulness. Then in the seventies a discovery was made. Enter the clitoral orgasm.

6. Women gained self-confidence in the assault on the double standard; and, for some, a new era of sexual enjoyment had arrived. But others found that adopting male attitudes to their sexual activity was unsatisfactory; their emotional requirements were left unsatisfied; they wanted men to love in a more intimate and caring way, like women. Furthermore, they found that men still designated them as "birds", "strokes", "tail", "broads", "pussy", and other degrading labels; and women whc 'slept around' were still "sluts".

7. Radical feminists maintained that men's sexuality was directed towards the conquest of women. Some saw intercourse as a political act of submission, and any dealings with men as traffic with, or giving succour to, the enemy. Hence the emergence of political lesbianism and separatism.

8. The uncovering of male violence towards women and the declaration "the personal is political".

9. The search continued for women's true sexuality - and men's. They found that women's sexuality is muted, diffuse, more sensual than a man's, and inextricably identified with love; that, for a woman, love is inseparable from emotion, tender and intimate; while love, for men, meant sexual activity, not necessarily involving any emotion.

17

Some of these discoveries were made during the early consciousness-raising sessions of the '70s, and others were the result of academic work. While more detailed studies, in subsequent years, uncovered new insights, these were made within that same basic framework.

Controversies broke out in defence of various theories: principally the one between biological determinism and cultural conditioning. Women are passive by nature, said the determinists. Women are not passive by nature, countered the cultural school, otherwise they would all be passive, just as, in principle, all women can have children; men are not dominant by nature, otherwise they would all be dominant, just as all men can have erections.

Internationally, various factions developed in feminism. There were those who believed in gradual reform so as not to antagonise men and the majority of women. Some visualised an androgynous type of equality and sexuality; and there were those who were prepared to fight on the barricades. For some (radical) feminists the barricades were drawn between the sexes and patriarchal heterosexuality became a target. A new category of sexual being emerged - political lesbians, women who refused to have sexual, or any other kind of relations with men. Political lesbianism was a rejection of heterosexuality, used as a tactic in the battle for equality, and not necesarily a positive desire for sexual engagement with women, or for freedom of sexual choice.

Some believed that the question of sexuality was overshadowing other pressing matters; that feminists were in danger of falling into a trap. They had protested against being cast as sex objects, yet they were involved in discussions of their sexuality to the point of obsession. Is sexuality really the arena, many asked, in which our well-being is determined in power-structures in modern society? What is the function of an ideology that keeps everyone looking for the meaning of life between their own or someone else's legs? On the contrary, said others, we have had our purpose in life tied to our sexuality; we have been made to suffer for it, and be ashamed of it, yet not allowed to enjoy it, or permitted to rise above a nearly exclusively sexual existence. We must understand our sexuality if we are to break free.

Later, other factions developed, including reactionary groups, such as cultural feminists who are defined differently in different countries. Their philosophy is basically opposed to the androgyny of earlier times. They celebrate the differences between women and men and believe that women's sexuality is biologically constructed (contradicting their title) and a resource rather than a handicap. Some want to return to the earlier values of respect for women, (which they say the sexual revolution destroyed), as a solution to male lasciviousness, dominance and violence. They want to encourage development of a women's culture separate from that of men, because they believe that men will never change.

While these discussions were engaging the minds and energies of feminists in other developed countries, things took a different turn in

Ireland. When internal tensions and personality differences broke up the Irish Women's Liberation Movement, some of the original members retired to work on their own lives in keeping with the motto, "the personal is political". You hear some of them now refer to a "post-feminist era". Some campaigned in the workplace, to ensure the implementation of equality and anti-discrimination legislation. Others sought, in the traditional caring role of women, to relieve the sufferings of women in particular situations of violence and oppression: battered women, rape victims, family planning and health. Difficult as it was, it was easier to struggle for equality in a series of specific battles against economic discrimination and violence than to challenge the deep cultural attitudes relating to sex. But general organisation of women to oppose their oppression, and the education of the mass of women, and of the next generation, eventually petered out.

While sexuality came out into the open in other societies, here it remained in the closet. Irish women (and men) have not involved themselves to any great extent in the agonising over sexuality which has occurred in other Western countries. While the feminist literature of other countries has endless dissertations on sexuality, discussion of the subject among Irish feminists was never able to surface into the public domain. Throughout this century, when research into sexuality became first a daring venture, and later became an accepted academic study, there was no public debate in this country on the theories of Freud (his name was whispered with prurient overtones), nor on the books of the sexologists - Kinsey, or Masters and Johnson, or Foucault, or Hite. These were all studies in one form or another of sexuality, female and male, and contributed to a better understanding of its complexity. Central to the deliberations of the sexologists was the vexed problem of the female orgasm. This elusive pimpernel was sought here, there and everywhere. With a seriousness that cannot but amuse, sexual gymnastics were devised to coax it out of hiding. Then, eureka, they discovered the clitoral orgasm. But wait! There was a snag! The clitoral orgasm was not dependent on penile penetration, or even on a man! A new theory of women's sexuality was emerging, inching slowly away from the male perspective.

DEFINING WOMEN'S SEXUALITY

Well what is the true definition of women's sexuality? The answer is that a woman's sexuality, and her physical enjoyment of it, has a much wider context than that defined as, or confined to, vaginal or clitoral orgasms, sexual intercourse, or erotic actions whether carried out alone or with another. The climax of female sexuality is giving birth, not intercourse which is only one milestone on the road to a woman's fulfilment. That is only the physical dimension. Manifestations of a woman's sexuality extend into her life in a way that influences all her behaviour and attitudes.

It is a cultural construct that birthing and child nurturing is divorced in our minds from sexual pleasure; that birth is associated with pain and treated as an illness. (By whom could it possibly be regarded as an illness except perhaps by men?) Some lucky women experience ecstatic physical pleasure in giving birth - those who are healthy and fit, and who go with the rhythms of labour rather than against them. Some women have experienced the paroxysm of delivery as an orgasm surpassing the genital one that gets such a high profile in the lexicon of sexual pleasure. *Giving birth is the logical climax in the essential sequence of a woman's sexuality, if one stops defining it in the male terms of intercourse.* It remains only for women to insist on conditions in the physical, social and political (the politics of the medicalisation of childbirth) environment of pregnancy and birth, and in the attitudes towards them, which would allow women to enjoy their pleasures.

This is not a new idea. I have come across it in feminist literature because I have been looking for it. On the zigzag path to awareness, it is easily missed if your mind is not open to it. Because motherhood has been used to suppress women, and has been a major factor in their oppression, many of the early feminists wanted to deny it, curtail it, excise it from the female consciousness. But, if I might be pardoned the pun, it was like throwing out the baby with the bath water.

Still, some recognised birthing for what it was. Dora Russell (1927) described intercourse for a woman as "the merest incident in the satisfaction of the older impulse to gain power and abundant and eternal life by multiplying her own body". When Germaine Greer (1984) saw the pleasure Tuscan women took in their children, and began to revise her earlier ideas about sexuality to include motherhood, she was castigated by less perceptive feminists, who had become entrenched at an earlier stage along the road of self-discovery. Mary Evans (1982), accused gynaecologists of practices "which, like those of pornography, (seem) incapable of seeing sexuality and reproduction as constituent elements of a complex system of responses". In *Our Bodies Ourselves*, by the Boston Women's Health Collective, the authors describe the second stage of labour as "joyful, not painful, to the overwhelming majority of women" even in the regular practice of routine obstetrics. Adrienne Rich quotes from several establishment researchers who have documented the erotic sensations experienced by women giving birth, and goes on to declare that there are strong cultural forces at work to desexualise women as mothers and to deny the orgasmic sensations felt in childbirth or while suckling infants. Today we might ask ourselves if the latent sexuality of childbirth and child nurturing has not had some part in the increasing numbers of single mothers raising their children.

It is true that birth has been strictly segregated from sexuality. In pregnancy and parturition women's sexual parts have been desexualised: the vagina becomes the birth canal. The atmosphere in a modern labour ward, the technology, the brisk impersonal attendants, the unnecessary use of drugs, also conspire to divorce childbirth from sexuality. It does not have to be like that; the current arrangements are solely for the convenience of the medical personnel. The up-ended-beetle position of the perinatal mother, lying on her back with her feet suspended in stirrups, allows medical personnel more ease of access to regulate the birth, often to suit their own purposes. Births are accomplished more easily for the mother if she squats, kneels or stands; yet few labour wards allow these positions.

Modern gynaecological and obstetrical practices, which historically have been oppressive and anti-woman, are male constructed. In the last century, male doctors displaced traditional midwives in what they undoubtedly saw as a lucrative field. Early on they developed anti-woman practices, such as clitoridectomy (yes, in civilised northern countries!) to cure female masturbation, and removal of the ovaries to cure insanity. These and other unbelievable surgical remedies were followed by manipulation of the birthing process: the more insidious one of drug administration, and routine, mechanical, and often unnecessary, interventions such as induction, forceps delivery, episiotomies and Caesarean sections, which continue to the present day. Women gynaecologists are trained by men and only a minority of them develop systems of their own, out of their own experience, like the English woman, Wendy Savage, who fell foul of the male gynaecological establishment for her woman-oriented practices.

Women cannot be blamed for experiencing childbirth as painful. Poor health, overwork, lack of fitness, bad posture, medical practices and cultural conditioning are basic causes of perinatal pain. The culture has decreed it; didn't God lay that curse on Eve in the Garden of Eden? Nobody has said that it need not be so, that giving birth can be a highly pleasurable part of their sexuality.

MALE SEXUALITY

If female sexuality is more than it is said to be, where then does that leave male sexuality? Well, for a start, it is much more narrowly defined than female sexuality. Men have a reductionist approach to sexuality, pruning it down to the bare essentials necessary for reproduction; but, paradoxically, engaging in the residual, perfunctory act principally for gratification. But is it the compulsive, aggressive, exploiting phenomenon that it is held to be? Many of us might say : no, not necessarily "aggressive" or "exploiting". "Compulsive"? Well, everyone knows that men's sex drive is a biological imperative, that they have no control over their erections. But is that a fact or merely an assumption?

One of the factors that cause differences between human sexuality and that of other mammals, as was said earlier, is human intelligence which regulates the instincts. Is male sexuality the only maverick instinct, unchecked by intellect? I think not. If that were so then no woman would ever be safe. Economic activity would grind to a halt; our workplaces would be snake pits of incapacitated males in the grip of engorged desire. No, our culture imposes limits which are invigilated by the intellect on the range of male sexuality. And from one culture to another there are different rules.

If a woman walks alone at night, if she dresses in what is deemed a "sexy" manner, she is said to be giving provocation to men, then she is to blame if she is attacked. (Shades of Adam and "it's all her fault"). In our society a glimpse of female breast can rouse a man; yet among some African tribes women go bare-breasted without causing a male flutter. If that is the case among primitive peoples, then breast fetishism, or arousal at the shape of the female figure or the sight of a woman alone, must be a learned response among our more cultivated and civilised tribesmen. Or, conversely, Africans have learned mammary indifference. One way or another there is a learning process. Furthermore, in our culture chastity is practiced among groups of men without undue physical stress (or else hordes of Roman Catholic priests are leading lives of rabid desperation). Obviously, they learn control of their sexuality. In millions of marriages men practice restraint, or have sexual equanimity that belies the idea of an uncontrollable biological imperative; but because of the cultural attitude towards male sexuality they would be slow to admit it. Sexual equanimity is unmanly; only the sexual activist can claim respect: 'A man's gotta do what a man's gotta do'.

If we can show, as I have just done, that there are cultural pressures on people to behave in a certain way, that the culture informs males that they should be excited by certain images, and in certain circumstances, then we cannot assume that sexual behaviour is only biological. It must be deduced logically that sexual responses can be learned and become cultural as well as biological imperatives. Therefore they can be unlearned. (I am not saying that cultural imperatives are always wrong. I only protest in this instance at carving them in stone, at misrepresenting male sexual responses as solely, unalterably biological.) And if male sexuality can be controlled by the intellect, as it undoubtedly can, then why in the name of sanity is it allowed untrammelled sway in relations between the sexes? Why has periodic male continence never been seriously considered in the context of contraception? The Rhythm and Billings methods of family planning are popularly derided as unworkable. The "biological compulsion" of male sexuality is given, and taken, as the reason why life is organised to provide a man with a regularly available woman, and why contraceptive devices are necessary if women are not to be eternally pregnant. To satisfy the importunate sexual demands of men, women have had to introduce hardware (sometimes lethal) into their bodies, and take drugs that are dangerous to their health, (consoled by doctors who say that on balance the risk is worth it). The answer is that men will not agree, and those who act reasonably and equitably don't publicly admit to it, and definitely don't urge that code of conduct on others. The myth of biological compulsion has been the single, greatest instrument for the sexual oppression of women; and, astonishingly, it has gone unchallenged, even in these comparatively enlightened, questing and questioning times.

WHERE DO WE GO FROM HERE?

It may seem glib to say, as some radical feminists have declared, that sexual violence and the sexual oppression of women are instruments of power that benefit all men, whether or not they are involved in their practice, or even approve of them. That may be so. Although there is no doubt that the subordination which results from the oppression of women at least satisfies male pride, and also provides them with personal service and support that smooths their way in life. But it is an unsatisfactory answer when one seeks ways to change prevailing attitudes. And how does one tackle the problem of misogyny when it is other women - secretaries, shop assistants, other men's partners, colleagues, cleaning women, "the woman in the street", old women, unmarried women - that men put down, generally not their own sisters, mothers, partners or daughters?

What can be done to change the situation? Many suggestions have been made, many policies tried. Political lesbians and cultural feminists have decided on courses of action; each in their own way have set about creating a culture which ignores male culture. For many that is not a realistic or feasible solution. Half the population of the planet is male, and most women find them interesting in themselves as well as necessary for procreation. Women also have sons.

There is another dimension to the matter: it would benefit men to shed some of their cultural conditioning, such factors as their martial rites, their power hunger and competitiveness; to free their emotions and learn to care; to share in the nurture of their children, whether or not it would affect the way their male offspring regard women. How can the mould be broken? A starting point could be, perhaps, if women tried to wean their children away from the worst excesses of male culture despite the pressures for young males to conform.

Should the family be abolished? It has come under fire from feminists as the locus of women's oppression; but what would replace it? Such an overwhelming majority of people find satisfaction and emotional security in the family that abolishing it is neither feasible nor desirable until a better structure can be devised. It can, however, be reformed into an institution that is user-friendly, especially to women.

I have shown that female and male sexuality have been distorted and restricted by the prevailing culture from their natural form. I make no claim to have discovered what the aggregate reality of that natural form is, beyond establishing that sexuality, as we interpret and know it, is distorted and stunted because it is used as an instrument of oppression.

It is warped and stunted because its definition is limited to the activity which constitutes the male role in reproduction, and which has been designated as the core of sexuality - a sexist definition and one that diminishes loving intimacy between people of either or the same sex, and denies the sexuality of giving birth. Homosexuality and self-stimulation are deprecated as unnatural and unclean. Childbirth becomes a medical problem; and both childbirth and child nurture are regarded as burdens.

This almost universally accepted definition of sexuality ignores, even denies, the reality of female sexuality which exists on a different plane and in a different dimension, to male experience. While female sexuality has been repressed, male sexuality has been allowed, indeed encouraged, to run rampant within its narrow definition, because masculinity is identified with sexuality. This restricted activity has become an addiction, men have developed into copulation junkies and they try to convince women that they should do the same.

In proposing that women set about changing the culture, are we seeking an unattainable Utopia? Perhaps. It takes an enormous internal struggle to change cultural attitudes in oneself without ever attempting to change the perceptions of others, especially sexual recidivists like men. It is easier for a subjugated group to recognise their oppression for what it is, than for the oppressors to admit, even to themselves, that they have fostered injustice, and constructed a culture and an interpretation of sexuality to support that injustice. On the other hand great strides have been made by women in the past twenty years in altering their perceptions of themselves and the world they live in.

The obsession of society with things sexual arises from several causes. An important one is the sexual oppression of women. With that, and one or two other causes out of the way, we could relegate sex to its rightful place in our lives - one that is neither obsessive nor neglected - and get on with the other exciting things there are to do, like changing the world and making it a better place for everyone.

REFERENCES

Boston Health Collective: *Our Bodies Ourselves,* Harmondsworth: Penguin; 1979. (Rev. edition, 1989)
Dinnerstein, Dorothy: *The Rocking of the Cradle and the Ruling of the World,* London: The Women's Press; 1987.
Rich, Adrienne: *Of Woman Born,* London: Virago; 1977.
Greer, Germaine: *Sex and Destiny,* London: Secker & Warburg; 1984.